MANAGING STRESS AND CONTROLLING SELF-DEFEATING BEHAVIOR

MANAGING STRESS AND CONTROLLING SELF-DEFEATING BEHAVIOR

CHARLES P. GILES, Ed.D.

National Publishers of the Black Hills, Inc.

Elmsford, NY

Cover and Interior Design: Hudson River Studio
Typesetting: Techna Type, Inc.
Editing and Production: Jane Andrassi and Ellen Schneid Coleman

CONTENTS

PREFACE

There is one basic assumption that you must accept if you are to get the most benefit from the lessons in this book. That assumption is that you *feel* the way you *think* and much of what you think is the result of a faulty premise. This means that you believe something that cannot be supported by facts. Such beliefs lead to conversations with yourself which are self-defeating because the self-dialogue sets you up to feel emotionally bad.

The self-defeating dialogue begins immediately after some initiating event occurs, to which you, based upon your *assessment* of that event, respond by telling yourself things that are not facts. But, since you believe them, you feel upset.

If you begin with the assumption that you are creating your depression, guilt, self-defeat, and so on by the way you think about an event, then the lessons that follow will teach you to begin managing stress and controlling self-defeating behavior.

A final reminder: self-diagnosis and treatment are not for everyone. Some people may need the help of a trained therapist to deal with their problems. However, self-management procedures help many people to feel better and cope better.

GLOSSARY

Below is a list of terms that will be used throughout this book. Look it over before you begin your study.

ACT STATEMENTS.   Statements that characterize events as "*Awful*," "*Catastrophic*," and/or "*Terrible*."

ALERT DIA-LOG.   Words that alert you to the fact that you are using stressful and defeating dialogue.

DEFEATING DIALOGUE.   Irrational, unprovable self-statements that usually result in inappropriate feelings with stressful and self-defeating outcomes.

DEFENSIVE DIALOGUE.   Rational, provable self-statements that usually lead to appropriate feelings, actively coping with a situation, and positive outcomes.

EVENT ASSESSMENT.   The way an individual evaluates an event that has led to a feeling. Assessment is *what* people tell themselves the event *means*. It is the interpretation of the initiating event.

FEELINGS.   The emotion created by the thought the individual has after assessing the event.

INITIATING EVENT.   Any situation which you believe activates or initiates an unsettling feeling, emotional upset, or stress.

IRRATIONAL BELIEFS.   Beliefs that cannot be proved, verified, or otherwise objectively supported with good evidence.

RATIONAL BELIEFS.   Beliefs that can be proved; beliefs for which there is acceptable, verifiable evidence.

SELF-DEFEATING BEHAVIOR.   Behavior that does not help a person to feel good, to love, to be satisfied and productive in work, to get along with others, to reduce stress, etc.

STRESS.   Anything that upsets psychological or physiological equilibrium or balance.

THOUGHTS.   Learned, automatic responses that occur after an individual assesses an event. Thoughts are reflected by one's inner talk.

YIT STATEMENTS.   Statements in which the individual blames everything on "You," "It," and/or "Them."

INTRODUCTION

The purpose of these learning units is to teach you to talk to yourself in ways that will increase your chances of managing stress and controlling self-defeating behavior. *Self-defeating behavior* is behavior that does not lead to outcomes that help you to feel better about yourself, to be satisfied and productive in your work, to love, to get along with others, to reduce stress, and to control other life situations. As a result, your chances of feeling good are reduced.

In fact, you have amazing control over the way you feel. This is because you feel what you think, and your thoughts are affected by the things you tell yourself. Your inner dialogue has a tremendous steering effect upon your emotional well-being. Since you have *learned* to talk to yourself in certain ways after you have evaluated a particular event in your life, you can also *learn* to assess events more objectively and learn to manage stress and defend yourself against defeating dialogue.

You are unique in this world. There has never been, there is not now, and there will never be another you. Furthermore, you are completely in charge of this unique you. To a very large extent, you determine the way you feel. Since you determine how you feel, it is in your best interest to feel *good*.

You can bring about dramatic changes in your life by learning the lessons that follow. By practice and persistence you will begin to defend yourself automatically against defeating dialogue, which you must give up if you want to manage stress and control self-defeating behavior.

Defensive dialogue is easy to learn and you will discover that it is a surprisingly effective way to control unsettling and upsetting emotions. The techniques you learn here will be habit forming. Unlike drugs, however, these habits will lead to pleasant results. Unlike dependence on chemicals, these habits are based on straight thinking, objective evaluation, and rational self-talk. We call it DEFENSIVE DIALOGUE.

This entire learning strategy was developed to help normal people (1) get in touch with the reasons behind most self-defeating behavior; (2) effectively and objectively evaluate any emotional feeling; (3) learn defensive dialogue to reduce stress, depression, and boredom; and (4) cope positively with life situations. If you are willing to make a commitment to practice and to persist, you can develop a new inner dialogue that will bring about pleasant changes in your life.

To begin, study the following statement: "I'm Going To Defend Myself Against Stress and Self-Defeating Behavior." If you believe that this is a worthy goal to which you can commit yourself, sign and date the pledge on page 3. It works best if you have a friend witness and sign the contract for you.

I'M GOING TO DEFEND MYSELF AGAINST STRESS AND SELF-DEFEATING BEHAVIOR

I've acquired some beliefs in my life that are unfortunate, unprovable, and unhealthy. They are self-defeating because they result in feelings, behavior, and inner dialogues that serve no purpose other than to make me feel bad. I don't like feeling bad—especially when this feeling is based on thinking that most probably is not true.

I'm going to stop rating the worth of myself and others. I'm going to stop telling myself that I *need* certain things in this world and *must* have them. I will no longer believe that you, it, or they *must* do, think, say, and act as I believe is absolutely necessary. I will stop telling myself that there are awful, terrible, horrible, and catastrophic events that compel me to feel depressed, anxious, jealous, frustrated, nervous, angry, bored, burned out, unproductive, and over-stressed. I should stop this defeating dialogue because it generates inappropriate feelings that make me feel bad.

Starting right now, I'm going to manage stress and control self-defeating behavior. I'm going to stop thinking and using defeating inner dialogue because it does not serve even one useful purpose. Not one! I'm going to start defending myself by replacing self-defeating thoughts and dialogue with rational thoughts and defensive dialogue. I'm going to learn *appropriate* feelings which are based on straight thinking. I'm going to *learn* defensive dialogue. Defensive dialogue, which is based on straight thinking and sound evidence, serves the most useful purpose in the world—*it makes me feel good!*

______________________   ______________________

Witness' signature   My signature

____

Historic date

THE DANGERS OF UNMANAGED STRESS

What does it mean to be sick? Are there any symptoms common to all disease? In exploring the meaning of "being sick," Dr. Hans Selye, one of the world's leading authorities on stress, has concluded that stress is the principal influence on *all* human behavior, whether in illness or in health. Dr. Selye has over a half century of laboratory research to back up his contention.

A major problem seems to be that every person inherits a limited amount of energy for adaptation to stress. What's more, whatever amount is used can't be replaced. When it's gone, it's gone! You can make withdrawals but no deposits.

Since we can't choose our parents, our best chance to live longer is to *manage well* what we have. I'm suggesting that we can probably control our longevity by learning techniques to manage stress effectively.

Stress is not all bad. Some stress is necessary to our well-being, and a lack of it can be harmful. Severe stress, however, is alleged to be a factor in such serious ailments as heart disease, high blood pressure, and stroke. The stress response is a primitive behavior held over from when man, faced with many dangers, had a fight or flight response. This response brings on certain physiological changes—blood sugar levels increase, pupils dilate so more light can be let in, and fatty acids such as cholesterol and triglycerides are released into the blood stream. These reflexes are necessary to prepare the body for action. But when this emergency preparation is excessive and lasts for long periods of time, it can become very dangerous. It can result in ulcers, hypertension (high blood pressure), heart disease, and stroke.

The program I recommend is dedicated to the control of stress. The proposition is that high levels of stress can be reduced. Furthermore, *avoiding* needless stress is a skill that can be *learned*. You can cope with stress by learning some methods to avoid and manage it. You will learn how to reorder your environment to minimize the frequency and effects of especially aggravating stress.

According to Dr. Hans Selye, normal human beings are generally prone to negative reactions to prolonged stress. He reports that there are about thirty-one signs of human response to stress ranging from depression to emotional tension, to insomnia, to neuroses, to psychoses, and more. Subjected to *either* extreme physical or psychological stress, the human body usually reacts with:

1. ALARM—an alarm response, followed by
2. RESISTANCE—a period of adaptation that continues until the body's vital energy is expended, followed by
3. EXHAUSTION—psycho-physical fatigue takes over the mind and body.

Dr. Selye calls this the General Adaptation Syndrome. A number of experts suspect that some individuals are more sensitive than others to physiological mechanisms of stress. Consequently, when these people become physiologically stressed it is highly likely that they will become psychologically (or emotionally) disturbed. A genetic or biological predisposition is an hereditary tendency toward development in a certain way. If an individual with such a predisposition is subjected to sufficient stress, physical disorders may develop.

Therefore, in any program of stress management it is important to learn both physiological and psychological techniques. It should also be emphasized that stress levels vary according to the individual, so it is important that people know their own level of stress. Every program of stress management is an individual endeavor.

Your first objective is to learn, "How do I know or recognize stress indicators in myself and others?" There are a number of signs of stress. Remember, each of us may respond—both outwardly and inwardly—with behavior that probably reflects a genetic predisposition. It is important to understand, therefore, that each of us will probably respond in our specific way, depending upon the weakest or most vulnerable part of our bodies. This physiological vulnerability may be a result of our inheritance.

How can you recognize stressors? Most people cannot, since the changes that stress causes in the mind and body are subtle and internal. Biofeedback machines help. Or you can *learn* to recognize certain behavior in yourself and others. Dr. Selye has found that most people tend to respond in one or more of the following ways:

- Irritability, hyper-excitation, or depression
- Pounding of the heart

- Dryness of throat, mouth
- Emotional instability, impulsive behavior
- Overpowering urge to run and hide
- Inability to concentrate
- Fatigue and loss of vigor
- Free-floating anxiety
- Emotional tension
- Stuttering, nervous tics, nervous laughter
- Inability to sleep
- Stomach problems
- Migraine headaches
- Increased use of tobacco, alcohol, drugs
- Neurotic behavior; psychoses

STRESS AND DISEASE

As you can see from this list, your emotions and stress are closely related. Emotional distress can be very dangerous! Physicians have suspected for years that chronic stress ultimately shortens your life.

The good news is that you can *learn* to *recognize, regulate,* and *reduce* the stressors in your life. Proper assessment of recent experiences is essential if you are to manage stress. Of course, a comprehensive stress management program includes exercise, diet, rest, and the elimination of high-risk behavior such as smoking, excessive drinking, and overeating.

The objective here is to help you learn techniques of *psychological* intervention that are effective in stress management. Stress, as used here, means anything that upsets psychological or physiological equilibrium or balance. Specifically, you will learn to control and manage stressors that result from the way you talk to yourself about events in your life.

Furthermore, it is extremely important to learn to control *excessive* stress. Why? Because excessive stress is a killer! You must learn to defend yourself against those things over which you *do* have control. Avoiding needless stress is a skill that can be learned, but you will need a great deal of practice, patience, and persistence to master it. If you want to cope with stress, this program will give you some pointers and some guidelines. Remember, you can learn to manage stress, but you must follow some rules—and practice!

Psychological stress has been linked to numerous illnesses, including insomnia and stroke, but in recent years most attention has focused on heart disease. Stress or frustration on the job or in personal or family life seems to increase the risk of coronary disease. The connection between stress and illness is especially marked when the source of stress (for example, being laid off from a job or the death of a close relative) is one over which a person has little or no control (Glass, 1977).

According to various studies, the person who runs the highest risk of heart disease is a man in his fifties who weighs too much and exercises too little; smokes more than a pack of cigarettes a day; has a high level of blood cholesterol; suffers from hypertension or diabetes; and has a family history of heart disease (Glass, 1977; Jenkins, 1971).

Underlying the various conditions that trigger heart disease is what Friedman and Rosenman (1974) call Type A behavior. Extreme Type A people are obsessed by a sense of the urgency of time and always try to do several things at once. They are frequently hostile and impatient, speak in staccato phrases, and often finish other people's sentences for them. They usually drive themselves harder at work than they do their employees; but, at the same time, they are competitive and difficult to get along with. Type B people, by contrast, are rarely driven to increase the amount of their output. Instead, they are concerned with the quality of achievement and experience. Often as intelligent and ambitious as their Type A counterparts, they frequently prevail over the more aggressive Type As.

Friedman and Rosenman found that the Type A men first studied in 1960 were nearly three times as likely as the Type B men to get heart disease during the next ten years. Glass suggests that Type As are especially sensitive to negative sources of stress that threaten their control over their environment. It appears that the response of Type As to such stressful life events increases their likelihood of heart disease (1977).

The relationship between stress and disease in human beings is still controversial. Some researchers continue to seek only physical causes of disease, but recent findings strongly suggest that both psychological and physical factors lie at the root of some of mankind's most troubling afflictions.

REFERENCES

Friedman, M., and R. H. Rosenman. *Type A Behavior and Your Heart*. New York: Knopf, 1974.

Glass, D. C. *Behavior Patterns, Stress and Coronary Disease*. New York: John Wiley, 1977.

Jenkins, C. D. "Psychologic and Social Precursors of Coronary Disease," *New England Journal of Medicine* (1971), pp. 284, 307–317.

Selye, Hans. *The Stress of Life*, rev. ed. New York: McGraw-Hill, 1976, pp. 174–177.

CONTRACTING

PURPOSE:
Signing a contract symbolizes your commitment to take action, to identify your goals, and to help you manage your time.

COMMITMENT

Stress management techniques can be learned, but strong commitment is required to build a successful stress management program. You will probably find that a contract is useful in starting and sustaining your program. The contract symbolizes your commitment, and helps you to define your goals, allot your time, and reward yourself for fulfilling the specifics of your contract. So we begin by introducing you to the concept of contracts.

You may find that a "contract" will help you begin, manage, and commit to a program of learning how to manage stress and control self-defeating behavior. It is recommended that you start each learning unit with a written contract acknowledging your commitment to the unit. These contracts will provide practice in defining your goals, will limit your specific learning task at each step, and will help you to manage and specify your time commitments.

It is best to tell another person of your decision for new learning. If you know that another person is aware of your decision, it will enhance your commitment and help you continue.

You will find examples of suggested contracts at appropriate places in this book. It is quite easy to add other desired behavioral changes to these contracts. You can easily learn to be an effective contract-maker. Remember, always be specific. Never make and sign a contract that does not at the very least indicate:

1. The behavior you are going to change. If several steps are involved, make a new contract for each step.
2. Exactly when you will begin (time, date).
3. Exact time and day of week for study, if appropriate.
4. Total weekly time you will devote to changing your behavior.
5. How you will reward yourself for completing the contract.
6. How you will penalize yourself if you do not live up to your contractual commitments.

Contracts and other self-commitments fail when the agreement is vague: to change "sometime," to practice "this week," or to do "something nice for myself" for trying.

CONTRACT FOR LEARNING THE DANGERS OF UNMANAGED STRESS

I agree to become aware of the dangers of unmanaged stress.

I will begin learning the dangers of unmanaged stress on (date): ____________________________________

I will complete my learning by (date): ____________________

My schedule will be as follows:
Days of the week I will study: ____________________

Time of day I will study: ____________________

Total time each week I will study: ____________________

My reward for completing the terms of my contract is:

____

My penalty for not completing the terms of my contract is:

____

____________________________   ____________________________

Witness' signature   My signature

                                                  ____

                                                  Date

CONTRACT FOR LEARNING TO MANAGE STRESS

I have decided to learn how to avoid needless stress. I realize that methods to avoid stress are skills that I can learn through practice. I will practice stress management skills on the following days and times:

Days: _______________________________________

Times: ______________________________________

I realize that the payoff for me is that the skills I learn will help me cope with stress through techniques that require no pills or other medication.

My reward for completing the terms of my contract is:

____

My penalty for not completing the terms of my contract is:

____

_________________________   _________________________
Witness' signature   My signature

                              ____
                                       Date

CONTRACT FOR LEARNING TO CONTROL
SELF-DEFEATING BEHAVIOR

I agree to learn how to control self-defeating behavior.

I will begin learning to control self-defeating behavior on
(date): ____

I will complete my learning by (date): _______________

My schedule will be as follows:
Days of the week I will study: _______________________

Time of day I will study: ____________________________

Total time each week I will study: ___________________

My reward for completing the terms of my contract is:

____

My penalty for not completing the terms of my contract is:

____

______________________________   ______________________

Witness' signature   My signature

                                                ____

                                                Date

ASSIGNMENT CONTRACT

I agree to practice and complete the following assignment.

I will begin on (date): _______________________________

I will finish on (date): ______________________________

The time of day I will study is: ______________________

The total time I will study is: _______________________

My present assignment is (write down the assignment in *detail*):

____

____

____

____

____

____

My reward for completing this assignment is:___________

____

My penalty for not completing this assignment is: _______

____

_______________________   _______________________
Witness' signature   My signature

                                ____
                                          Date

REWARD AND PENALTY LISTS

Immediately after signing your contract, begin to think about rewards and penalties. The purpose of reward and penalty lists is to have a group of rewards available to expedite the completion of your contract and a list of penalties that would result should you fail to complete your assignment.

Remember, you may choose one of the rewards *only* when you successfully complete an assignment. The items on your reward list are available to you *only* by doing. They are contingent upon accomplishing what you have contracted to do! (As you can see, the lack of reward may become, in fact, a penalty.)

Your penalty list contains specific things that you do not like to do, but *must* do if you fail to complete the assignment.

Now, spend several minutes compiling your reward and penalty lists. *Do not stop* until you have your lists!

REWARD LIST	PENALTY LIST
A reward is something very special you do for yourself. Examples are TV time, food, music, sports, holiday—YOU decide.	A penalty is something you *really* dislike. It could be denying yourself a reward, or something like mowing the lawn, cleaning house, or contributing money.

Below is an example of a rewards and penalties list:

POTENTIAL REWARDS *(a shopping list)*	POTENTIAL PENALTIES *(a "disgusting" list)*
Money	Clean house/yard/garage/ attic
Food	Get up at 5:00 A.M. to study
Drink	
Sleeping late	
Ticket to concert, sporting event, etc.	Give up ___________
Clothes	Can't go to ___________
Household items (rugs, furniture, TV, etc.)	
Sport/Hobby equipment	Walk instead of drive for one day

Listening to stereo	Do twenty pushups
Watching TV	Attend ___________,
Taking a trip	which I HATE!
Free time	Do without something I
Party	have listed as a reward
Swim	Donate $20.00 to an
Fishing/Hunting/Camping	organization I dislike

CHECKLIST

Below are the things you should know by now. *Check* yourself and be sure you have completed all of the previous learning assignments before you proceed. The payoff for your work is managing stress, controlling self-defeating behavior, and feeling good. Sign the following statement:

I understand that I cannot proceed until all blanks are checked.

_________________________________   _________________________________

Signature   Date

___________ I know that I feel the way I think.

___________ I know that I have control over my feelings.

___________ I can learn defensive dialogue which will help me manage stress and control self-defeating behavior.

___________ I am going to defend myself against stress and self-defeating behavior.

___________ I know some definitions, or I know how to look up unfamiliar terms in the *Glossary*.

__________ I have signed contracts to learn how to manage stress and control self-defeating behavior.

__________ I agree to practice, persist, be patient, and complete my learning assignments.

__________ I have compiled my reward and penalty lists.

THOUGHTS, FEELINGS, AND IRRATIONAL IDEAS

PURPOSE:
To learn to distinguish between thoughts and feelings and to become aware of the most common irrational thoughts and ideas.

Around the first century A.D. the Greek philosopher Epictetus said: "People are disturbed not by things, but by the views they take of them."

A few centuries later Shakespeare, in *Hamlet*, said: "There is nothing either good or bad, but thinking makes it so."

In this section you will begin to examine how thinking affects feelings. You will start to learn that you can distinguish between your thoughts and your feelings (as, indeed, you must). When you learn to tune into your thoughts and see that it is what you *think* about an event that causes your feeling, you will understand that the things you *tell* yourself can be self-defeating.

You are about to learn to change your inner dialogue. You will discover that when you feel extremely upset because of something you have just told yourself, then the dialogue is probably defeating. Because you are in control of your inner dialogue, you can defend yourself by learning to use defensive dialogue.

CONTRACT FOR ASSIGNMENT 1:
DISTINGUISHING BETWEEN
THOUGHTS AND FEELINGS

I agree to practice and complete Assignment 1.

____

I will begin on (date): _______________________

I will finish on (date): ______________________

The time of day I will study is: ______________
(Recommended time: one day for one hour.)

My reward for completing this assignment is: __________

____

My penalty for not completing this assignment is: _______

____

_________________________   ________________________
Witness' signature   My signature

                                 ____
                                        Date

ASSIGNMENT 1: DISTINGUISHING BETWEEN THOUGHTS AND FEELINGS

1. I *feel* the way I *think.*
    a. I will learn to tune into my thoughts.
    b. I will learn to distinguish between my *thoughts* and
       my *feelings.*

2. I will learn to identify a corresponding negative or irrational *thought* when I become upset about something.
3. The actual events that occur do not result in my mood changes and self-defeating behavior. Rather, my perception (what I *think*) of those events causes me to feel an emotion such as anger, happiness, fear, depression, boredom, burnout, etc. I understand that this is what takes place:
   a. Something happens (an initiating event) at home, work, etc.
   b. I assess that event, and automatically talk to myself using dialogue I have learned to believe is appropriate in this situation.
   c. My feelings are the result of my thoughts and self-talk, *not* the actual event.
   d. If my thoughts and inner dialogue are rational and positive, my emotions will be normal and appropriate.
   e. If my thoughts are irrational and negative, my dialogue will be abnormal, inappropriate, and self-defeating.
4. I know that unpleasant feelings may show that I am thinking negatively, using defeating dialogue.
5. Just because I *feel* something doesn't make it a *fact*.
6. My objective is to learn appropriate emotions, not to become emotion-*less*.

I realize that to control self-defeating behavior, I must diligently complete my homework, and practice, persist, and be patient.

CONTRACT FOR ASSIGNMENT 2:
THOUGHTS PLUS SELF-TALK

I agree to practice and complete Assignment 2.

____

I will begin on (date): _______________________________

I will finish on (date): ___________________________

The time of day I will study is: ___________________
(Recommended time: one day for one hour.)

My reward for completing this assignment is: _________

____

My penalty for not completing this assignment is: ______

____

_________________________   _________________________
Witness' signature   My signature

                                      ____
                                      Date

ASSIGNMENT 2: THOUGHTS PLUS SELF-TALK

OBJECTIVE: To learn to distinguish between *thoughts* and *feelings*.

THOUGHTS: You will become aware of thoughts by listening to how you talk to yourself. Therefore, we will define a thought as your internal *dialogue*. Thoughts are *learned* responses and occur almost instantaneously. They are triggered by initiating events. They are what you think at the moment. Your inner talk reflects what you are thinking; for example, "This job is awful and terrible and boring."

FEELINGS: A feeling is created by your thoughts and self-talk. Feelings can generally be defined in terms of an emotion, such as fear, happiness, depression, sadness, anxiety, anger, etc. The "way you take it" and what you say to yourself determines the feeling. The feeling from thinking, "This job is awful and terrible and boring," may be depression, lethargy, even anger.

THOUGHT PLUS SELF-TALK	*POTENTIAL FEELING*
"Everyone dislikes me."	Depression
"She/He shouldn't say those things to me!"	Anger; self-pity
"I never do anything right, so why should I try?"	Depression; self-pity; helplessness
"They are challenging my beliefs."	Anxiety; fear
"I'll never find another love."	Depression
"I can't *stand* this job!"	Lethargy; depression

As you can see, these thoughts and self-talk lead to negative feelings.

CONTRACT FOR ASSIGNMENT 3:
THE RELATIONSHIP OF
POSITIVE AND NEGATIVE THOUGHTS TO BELIEFS

I agree to practice and complete Assignment 3.

____

I will begin on (date): _______________________________

I will finish on (date): _______________________________

The time of day I will study is: _______________________
(Recommended time: one day for one hour.)

My reward for completing this assignment is: ___________

____

My penalty for not completing this assignment is: _______

Witness' signature	My signature
	Date

ASSIGNMENT 3: THE RELATIONSHIP OF POSITIVE AND NEGATIVE THOUGHTS TO BELIEFS

OBJECTIVE: To learn the relationship of positive and negative thoughts to beliefs.

You have been practicing techniques to help you distinguish thoughts from feelings. Now that you can do this, you should learn more about *positive* and *negative* thoughts.

Both *positive* and *negative* thoughts are related to your *beliefs*.

Negative thoughts usually result from *irrational* beliefs. They have no basis in fact. They can't be proved. They are distorted and unverifiable. They are learned. Negative thoughts are *self-defeating* thoughts.

No one but you can control your thinking processes. Telling yourself things that are probably very questionable serves no useful purpose. It is not in your best interest to think irrationally. Irrational notions will do you in. Defeating dialogue, if not challenged and changed, will eventually create its own reality. Defeating dialogue is your enemy because it causes anxiety, depression, rage, fear, failure, and putting yourself down. Defeating dialogue inhibits success, love, productivity, self-esteem, and feeling good.

Positive thoughts usually result from *rational* beliefs. They are factual, provable, and verifiable. Positive thinking can be *learned*. Positive thinking leads to appropriate feelings, rational behavior, and the ability to cope with situations in healthy ways.

Your thoughts create your feelings. Unpleasant feelings

may indicate that you are having negative and irrational thoughts—and *believing* them.

Memorize this sentence—*right now!* Positive thoughts help you evaluate and assess a situation properly, to respond appropriately to events, and change the situation if necessary.

David Burns, M.D., in his book *Feeling Good: The New Mood Therapy*,[1] identifies ten thought distortions that he believes significantly affect our behavior. For example, Dr. Burns believes that we tend to see things in black and white categories, such as, bad things *"always* happen to me," or "I *never* win." We also tend to reject positive experiences and maintain negative beliefs; we overgeneralize negative events and assume the situation will never change; we latch onto "shoulds" and "should nots"; we assume that negative emotions are proof of the way things really are. These and other thought distortions, Dr. Burns contends, result in our not feeling good about ourselves.

The outstanding psychotherapist, Dr. Albert Ellis, in his book *A New Guide To Rational Living*,[2] (with R. A. Harper) maintains that there are several powerful and irrational ideas that stand in the way and present us from leading a pleasant emotional life. Among these are the notions that we *must* have love and approval, that emotional misery is caused by outside forces and, therefore, we have little control over our feelings, that things *should* turn out better for us, and that we have to view frustrating things as terrible and awful.

CONTRACT FOR ASSIGNMENT 4:
DR. DAVID BURNS'S TEN THOUGHT DISTORTIONS
AND DR. ALBERT ELLIS'S IRRATIONAL IDEAS

I agree to practice and complete Assignment 4.

____

I will begin on (date): _______________________________

I will finish on (date): _______________________________

The time of day I will study is: ________________________
(Recommended time: one day for one hour.)

My reward for completing this assignment is: ___________

____

My penalty for not completing this assignment is: ________

____

________________________   ________________________

   Witness' signature   My signature

                                  ____

                                            Date

ASSIGNMENT 4: DR. DAVID BURNS'S TEN THOUGHT DISTORTIONS AND DR. ALBERT ELLIS'S IRRATIONAL IDEAS

OBJECTIVE: To learn the Ten Thought Distortions and the Irrational Ideas.

TEN THOUGHT DISTORTIONS

1. *ALL-OR-NOTHING THINKING:* You see things in black-and-white categories. If your performance falls short of perfect, you see yourself as a total failure.
2. *OVERGENERALIZATION:* You see a single negative event as a never-ending pattern of defeat.
3. *MENTAL FILTER:* You pick out a single negative detail and dwell on it exclusively so that your vision of all reality becomes darkened, like the drop of ink that discolors the entire beaker of water.
4. *DISQUALIFYING THE POSITIVE:* You reject positive experiences by insisting they "don't count" for some

reason or other. In this way you can maintain a negative belief that is contradicted by your everyday experiences.

5. *JUMPING TO CONCLUSIONS:* You make a negative interpretation even though there are no definite facts that convincingly support your conclusion.
   a. *Mind reading.* You arbitrarily conclude that someone is reacting negatively to you, and don't bother to check this out.
   b. *The Fortune Teller Error.* You anticipate that things will turn out badly, and you feel convinced that your prediction is an already-established fact.

6. *MAGNIFICATION (CATASTROPHIZING) OR MINIMIZATION:* You exaggerate the importance of things (such as your goof-up or someone else's achievement), or you inappropriately shrink things until they appear tiny (your own desirable qualities or the other fellow's imperfections). This is also called the "binocular trick."

7. *EMOTIONAL REASONING:* You assume that your negative emotions necessarily reflect the way things really are: "I feel it, therefore it must be true."

8. *SHOULD STATEMENTS:* You try to motivate yourself with shoulds and shouldn'ts, as if you had to be whipped and punished before you could be expected to do anything. "Musts" and "oughts" are also offenders. The emotional consequence is guilt. When you direct should statements toward others, you feel anger, frustration, and resentment.

9. *LABELING AND MISLABELING:* This is an extreme form of overgeneralization. Instead of describing your error, you attach a negative label to yourself: "I'm a loser." When someone else's behavior rubs you the wrong way, you attach a negative label to him: "He's a louse." Mislabeling involves describing an event with language that is highly colored and emotionally loaded.

10. *PERSONALIZATION:* You see yourself as the cause of some negative external event which in fact you were not primarily responsible for.

According to Dr. Ellis, several powerful and irrational ideas prevent your leading an anxiety-free, unhostile life.

IRRATIONAL IDEAS

IRRATIONAL IDEA No. 1.   The idea that you *must* have love or approval from all the people you find significant.

IRRATIONAL IDEA No. 2.   You must prove thoroughly competent, adequate, and achieving (or a saner but still foolish variation: the idea that you at least must have competence or talent in some important area).

IRRATIONAL IDEA No. 3.   The idea that when people act obnoxiously and unfairly, you should blame and damn them, and see them as bad, wicked, or rotten individuals.

IRRATIONAL IDEA No. 4.   The idea that you have to view things as awful, terrible, horrible, and catastrophic when you get seriously frustrated, are treated unfairly, or are rejected.

IRRATIONAL IDEA No. 5.   The idea that if something seems dangerous or fearsome, you must preoccupy yourself with it and make yourself anxious about it.

IRRATIONAL IDEA No. 6.   The idea that emotional misery comes from external pressures and that you have little ability to control or change your feelings.

IRRATIONAL IDEA No. 7.   The idea that you can more easily avoid facing many life difficulties and self-responsibilities than undertake more rewarding forms of self-discipline.

IRRATIONAL IDEA No. 8.   The idea that your past remains all-important and that because something once strongly influenced your life, it has to keep determining your feelings and behavior today.

IRRATIONAL IDEA No. 9.   The idea that people and things should turn out better than they do and that you must view it as awful and horrible if you do not find good solutions to life's grim realities.

IRRATIONAL IDEA No. 10.   The idea that you can achieve maximum human happiness by inertia and inaction or by passively and uncommittedly "enjoying yourself."

CHECKLIST

I have completed or agree to complete the following learning assignments. I understand I cannot proceed until all the blanks are checked.

______________________   ______________________

         Signature   Date

__________ I believe thinking affects my feelings.

__________ I know that my inner dialogue reflects my thoughts.

__________ I know that I feel the way I think.

__________ I know the difference between thoughts and feelings.

__________ I know that positive and negative thoughts are related to what I believe.

__________ I am familiar with David Burns's ten thought distortions and Albert Ellis's list of irrational ideas.

NOTES
1. New York: New American Library, 1980, pp. 40–41.
2. Hollywood, Calif.: Wilshire Book Co., Copyright 1975 by the Institute For Rational Emotive Therapy, Albert Ellis, Executive Director.

USING THE DAILY DIA-LOG TO RECOGNIZE STRESSORS AND ASSESS EVENTS

PURPOSE:
To learn (1) how to keep and use a DAILY DIA-LOG
(2) why the log is necessary
(3) how to log and assess stressors and upsetting events

RECOGNIZING STRESSORS

It is difficult to deal with any behavior until you first identify the behavior with which you want to cope. Therefore, you must first identify the stressors present in your everyday life. Second, you must become aware of how these stressors affect you, and how they relate to your thinking processes.

STEP 1: Take the two short tests on pages 33, 34 and 35 to gauge your physical and mental stress and tension levels. Do not proceed until you have taken these tests.

STEP 2: Sign a contract—right now—committing yourself to recognizing stressors.

STEP 3: Learn to identify potential stressors by keeping a log of sources of stress and your responses to those sources. In this learning exercise, you will begin to log *what happened* to cause you stress, what you *said to yourself* about the stress-initiating event (*defeating dialogue*), and to replace what you say to yourself with more appropriate self-talk (*defensive dialogue*).

The ability to predict a stressor is very important because predictability can lessen the stressor's effects. If you know the signals that a stressor is threatening, and how regularly it occurs, the results will be less harmful.

CONTRACT FOR LEARNING HOW TO RECOGNIZE STRESSORS

I agree to learn how to recognize stressors.

I will begin learning how to control stressors on (date):

____

I will complete my learning by (date):   _______________

My schedule will be as follows:
Days of the week I will study are: _______________

Time of day I will study: _______________________

Total time each week I will study: _______________

My reward for completing the terms of my contract is:

____

My penalty for not completing the terms of my contract is:

____

_______________________   _______________________
Witness' signature   My signature

                                                ____
                                                Date

TEST 1: THE SOCIAL READJUSTMENT RATING SCALE[1]

Instructions: Add up the value of Life Crisis Units for Life Events experienced in two-year period.

Life Event	*Life Crisis Units*
1. Death of a spouse	100
2. Divorce	73
3. Marital separation	65
4. Jail term	63
5. Death of close family member	63
6. Personal injury or illness	53
7. Marriage	50
8. Fired at work	47
9. Marital reconciliation	45
10. Retirement	45
11. Change in health of family member	44
12. Pregnancy	40
13. Sex difficulties	39
14. Gain of new family member	39
15. Business readjustment	39
16. Change in financial state	38
17. Death of a close friend	37
18. Change to a different line of work	36
19. Change in number of arguments with spouse	35
20. Mortgage over $40,000	31
21. Foreclosure of mortgage or loan	30
22. Change in responsibilities at work	29
23. Son or daughter leaving home	29
24. Trouble with inlaws	29
25. Outstanding personal achievement	28
26. Wife begins or stops work	26
27. Begin or end school	26
28. Change in living conditions	25
29. Revision of personal habits	24
30. Trouble with boss	23
31. Change in work hours or conditions	20
32. Change in residence	20

33. Change in schools	20
34. Change in recreation	19
35. Change in church activities	19
36. Change in social activities	18
37. Mortgage or loan less than $40,000	17
38. Change in sleeping habits	16
39. Change in number of family get-togethers	15
40. Change in eating habits	15
41. Vacation	13
42. Christmas	12
43. Minor violations of the law	11

0 to 150—No significant problems
150 to 199—Mild life crisis (33% chance of illness)
200 to 299—Moderate life crisis (50% chance of illness)
300 or over—Major life crisis (80% chance of illness)

*TEST 2: QUICK-SCORING TEST FOR ASSESSING STRESS AND TENSION LEVELS**

Circle the answer at right that applies most to you.

	VERY OFTEN	*3 OR MORE TIMES A WEEK*	*HARDLY EVER*
1. I just can't seem to find the time to relax.	2	1	0
2. Even when I find the time, I can't seem to relax or sleep.	2	1	0

*This test is for self-assessment only. Its diagnostic validity has not been established and the test should be used only to estimate a person's self-perceived tension level.

3. I find it necessary to take medication or drugs to relax.	2	1	0
4. Meeting deadlines is something I face every day.	2	1	0
5. I find it difficult to concentrate because of all the worries I have.	2	1	0
6. I feel anxious, uptight, or have pain in my neck and shoulders.	2	1	0
7. I have severe headaches or a nervous stomach.	2	1	0
8. When I'm tense, I drink/take drugs/ smoke more.	2	1	0
9. People make me tense.	2	1	0
10. Even when I'm not working, I have difficulty clearing my mind enough to relax.	2	1	0

TOTAL SCORE

SCORE	TENSION LEVEL
14–18	Above average
10–13	Somewhat above average
6–9	Average
3–5	Somewhat below average
0–2	Below average

LOGGING AND EVENT ASSESSMENT

Keeping a daily log of the stressors and the unsettling events in your life serves two primary purposes. First, recording the events that upset you tends to increase your awareness of what is happening. Second, logging is an extremely effective method of getting yourself used to recognizing the automatic thoughts and self-talk that follow an initiating event.

"Unsettling," "disturbing," or "upsetting" events are *any* events that affect how you function in a given situation. It can be something that someone says to you that suddenly makes you feel angry and hostile, or rejected and depressed, or any of a host of other feelings. It can be a feeling you get just before you make a speech or call on a customer that makes you decide not to follow through.

The importance of logging every disturbing event cannot be overemphasized. It is absolutely necessary to write down these events if you are to learn how to use defensive dialogue. Later, of course, you will not write down disturbing events. Instead, you will automatically go through the learned thinking process.

Objectivity is very important in assessing the events that activate your thoughts and feelings. If you are to manage stress and control self-defeating behavior, you must learn to assess an event objectively, logically, and rationally. How you assess an event is a product of your thought system and leads to either defeating or defensive dialogue.

You will be richly rewarded in a relatively short time if you begin first to log and then to assess every disturbing, unsettling, or upsetting event.

KEEPING AND USING A DAILY DIA-LOG

A necessary step in learning to manage stress and control self-defeating behavior is to become aware of your thoughts and inner talk. The purpose of keeping the DAILY DIA-LOG is (1) to get in the habit of logging the events of your day which seem to initiate unsettling and upsetting emotional responses, (2) to evaluate those events objectively, and (3) to learn defensive talk to prevent results that are harmful to you.

During the first week of this learning assignment the only requirement is to log the initiating event that you believe is the cause of your disturbed feeling. For example, suppose your boss expresses disappointment with some of your work and you are upset. You think that your boss is being unduly critical of you. Log only the event (what the boss said). *Do not log the thought* ("The boss is being critical of me.") This is how to log the event:

WHAT HAPPENED
(initiating event)

---

1. Boss expressed disappointment with my work.

Other examples of initiating events:

- "My coworkers went to lunch and didn't invite me."
- "I dread entering the place I work."
- "The person in front of me is driving too slow."
- "My friend rejected me."
- "A coworker said I was buttering up the boss."

The idea is to get into the habit of recording *what happened*, or the initiating event. After a week of logging initiating events you will be familiar with the first entry in your DAILY DIA-LOG. Complete the following contract *now*.

CONTRACT FOR ASSIGNMENT 1:
DAILY DIA-LOG

I agree to keep a daily log of all events that happen just before I have upsetting or unsettling feelings.

I will begin keeping my log on (date): _______________________

I will keep my log for at least one week, which will end on

(date): _______________________

My reward for completing this assignment is: ___________

____

My penalty for not completing this assignment is: _______

____

Additional commitments are (write none if none): _______

____

_______________________   _______________________
      Witness' signature   My signature

                              ____
                                        Date

ASSIGNMENT 1: DAILY DIA-LOG

WHAT HAPPENED (the initiating event): Write down initiating events as they happen. Write down *only* what happened.

1. ____

____

2. ____

____

3. ____

____

4. ____

____

5. ____

   ____

6. ____

   ____

7. ____

   ____

8. etc.

Note: Do not continue your study until you have practiced this assignment for at least one week.

CONTRACT FOR ASSIGNMENT 2:
LOGGING AND ASSESSING EVENTS

I agree to keep a daily log of events I find upsetting and my assessment of each event.

I will begin keeping my log on (date): _______________

I will keep my log for at least one week, which will end on

(date): _______________________

My reward for completing this assignment is: _______

____

My penalty for not completing this assignment is: _______

____

_______________________   _______________________

     Witness' signature   My signature

                                        ____

                                          Date

ASSIGNMENT 2: LOGGING AND ASSESSING EVENTS

Note: Begin this assignment *only* after you have logged initiating events for *at least* one week.

You are now routinely logging the upsetting events in your daily life. Your next assignment is to write down in your log *what you say to yourself* following the events that you find upsetting. This will help you get in touch with what you *automatically think* after the event.

You will now begin to keep a two-column log. The two-column log should be maintained for *at least* one week. One week of practice should get you into the habit of recording. Soon the process will become routine.

In the *first column* of your log, record the event that was unsettling, upsetting, disturbing, etc.—just as you did in Assignment 1 of this unit. Use as few words as possible, but try to be specific.

When something happens immediately tell yourself what it *means.* That is, interpret or *assess* the event. In the *second column* write down your interpretation, evaluation, or *assessment* of the event. For now, all you need to do is write *what* you believe or think the event *means.* These assessments are your very first, automatic thoughts about what happened. Write them down because the assessment you make creates the feeling or emotion that follows the event. Your only concern is (1) to log the event or what happened, and (2) to assess what the event *means.*

Following are some examples of how to use the two-column log.

DAILY DIA-LOG

WHAT HAPPENED *(initiating event)*	WHAT I SAID TO MYSELF *(my inner dialogue)*

1. The boss expressed disappointment with my work.

   1. "My boss is being awfully critical of me.
   or
   "I guess I'm no good at this job."
   or
   "How dare that _______ say that to me!"

2. I am in a traffic jam going to work.

   2. "The dumb drivers in this town don't know how to drive!"
   or
   "GET OUT OF THE WAY! YOU are making me late for work."
   or
   "I can't stand this traffic any longer."

3. I am rejected by someone.

   3. "I can't stand it that I have been rejected. No one should do that to me."

DAILY DIA-LOG

WHAT HAPPENED *(initiating event)*	WHAT I SAID TO MYSELF *(my inner dialogue)*

1. _______________________

1. _______________________

2. _______________________   2. _______________________

3. _______________________   3. _______________________

4. _______________________   4. _______________________

5. _______________________   5. _______________________

6. _______________________   6. _______________________

7. _______________________   7. _______________________

8. _______________________   8. _______________________

9. _______________________________   9. _______________________________

   _______________________________   _______________________________

   _______________________________   _______________________________

10. _______________________________   10. _______________________________

   _______________________________   _______________________________

   _______________________________   _______________________________

You may use the same technique to log stress and tension. Below is an example of how to log stressors.

DAILY STRESS AND TENSION LOG

What Happened (Stressor)	Time of Day	What I Said to Myself	How I Felt	My Response (Behavior)
Example: I had a deadline that I didn't meet.	11 A.M.	"I knew I'd never do this on time."	Very Anxious	Gave Excuses

Keep the log for at least one week. After a week or so of logging stressors you will begin to recognize the things in your life that produce stress. You will probably discover that your responses are self-defeating and stressful. It is in your best interest, therefore, to make the changes necessary to control your stress. You will learn how to do this in the lessons beginning on page 63.

Make a five-column log on a piece of plain paper. Keep a daily log of (1) what happens, (2) what time of day it happens, (3) what you say to yourself when it happens, (4) how you feel when it happens, and (5) your response, or behavior, to what happens.

DAILY STRESS AND TENSION LOG

What Happened (Stressor)	Time of Day	What I Said to Myself	How I Felt	My Response (Behavior)

CHECKLIST

I have completed or agree to complete the following learning assignments. I understand I cannot proceed until all the blanks are checked.

_______________________________ _______________________________
          Signature   Date

_________ I understand that I need to identify the stressors in my everyday life.

_________ I understand that I need to become aware of how these stressors affect me and how they relate to my thinking processes.

_________ I will take the two short tests on pages 33, 34, and 35.

_________ I will sign a contract to learn how to recognize stressors.

_________ I understand the two primary purposes of keeping a daily log of stressors and unsettling or upsetting events.

_________ I will keep a daily log of stressors and disturbing events.

_________ I will begin to assess each initiating event and write down what I think that event means.

_________ I understand and will follow the instructions on how long to continue my log.

_________ I know I have everything to gain and nothing to lose by persisting in my efforts to manage stress and control self-defeating behavior.

_________ I know I must practice, persist, and be patient.

NOTES

1.   T.H. Holmes and R.H. Rake, "The Social Readjustment Rating Scale," *Journal of Psychosomatic Research* 11 (1967) 213–218.

RECOGNIZING AND CHALLENGING DEFEATING DIALOGUE

PURPOSE:
To learn to define, recognize, and challenge defeating dialogue.

You have now learned to *recognize stressors*, to log *what happened*, and to *assess what happened* and *what you said to yourself* about what happened. You have also learned about *thoughts, self-talk, and feelings.* You will now learn to evaluate your self-talk and determine if what you tell yourself is defeating dialogue. *Memorize* the definition of defeating dialogue.

> Defeating dialogue is irrational, unprovable self-statements a person makes that very probably will result in inappropriate feelings with self-defeating outcomes.

If you use defeating dialogue, you must defend yourself, or the outcome will be self-defeating.

The next step in managing stress and controlling self-defeating behavior is learning to recognize defeating dialogue and replace it with defensive dialogue.

CONTRACT FOR RECOGNIZING
DEFEATING DIALOGUE

I agree to memorize the criteria for determining if my self-talk is defeating dialogue. I will limit myself to two days for this learning assignment.

I will begin this assignment on (date): _________________

I will complete this assignment by (date): _______________

Time of day I will study: _______________________

My reward for completing the terms of my contract is:

____

My penalty for not completing the terms of my contract is:

____

_______________________   _______________________
Witness' signature   My signature

                                        ____
                                                    Date

DETERMINING WHEN DIALOGUE IS DEFEATING

Dialogue is defeating when it:

1. Does not realistically and accurately assess the initiating event.
2. Is life threatening.

3. Decreases an individual's chances of getting along with other people.
4. Increases the probability that an individual will become emotionally upset, and, as a result, less productive.
5. Commands, demands, and judges.
6. Severely limits an individual's options to change and reach goals.

Do not continue until you have learned these six rules. These general rules are important, and are even more helpful when combined with the following five additional definitions of defeating dialogue.

1. Defeating dialogue follows from unrealistic or irrational thinking. It is probably based on poor evidence, or a faulty premise, and often grossly overgeneralizes the situation. "I just can't stand it if my friend rejects me." "It is just terrible that so-and-so said that awful thing to me."
2. Defeating dialogue often reflects demands upon others and/or the environment. "YIT *must*." (You must; It must; They must). "Since I can't stand it if my friend rejects me, he/she must not."
3. Defeating dialogue leads to inappropriate and disturbing emotions. If your friend is going to reject you and never see you again, you may say to yourself (1) "Who cares? It isn't important and matters little to me," or (2) "There must be something bad about me." Either statement decreases the likelihood that you will cope with the situation positively and increases the probability that you will feel apathetic or anxious. It is highly unlikely that either statement is true, and both only lead to distressing feelings.
4. Defeating dialogue does not move you toward your goal of relative happiness.
5. Defeating dialogue decreases your chances to feel good and live productively.

Study these five statements until you are thoroughly familiar with them. Quiz yourself.

CONTRACT FOR ASSIGNMENT 1:
RECOGNIZING SELF-DEFEATING TERMS

I agree to practice and complete Assignment 1.

____

I will begin on (date): _______________________

I will finish on (date): _______________________

Time of day I will study: _______________________

My reward for completing this assignment is: _______

____

My penalty for not completing this assignment is: _______

____

_______________________   _______________________
Witness' signature   My signature

                                 ____
                                         Date

ASSIGNMENT 1: RECOGNIZING SELF-DEFEATING TERMS

Continue to keep a DAILY DIA-LOG of what happens and your assessment of what happens. This assignment will help you become aware of, or alerted to, self-defeating terms you use.

Follow these steps for this assignment:

1. Learn the terms in column one of the ALERT DIA-LOG on page 52.
2. Then go back to the DAILY DIA-LOG you have been keeping and, in column two of the ALERT DIA-LOG, enter the *number of times* you have used the term.
3. In the third column of the ALERT DIA-LOG write "I," "You," "It," or "They" ("Them") if the term was *preceded* by, or used in conjunction with, any of the four.

Practice for at least seven days. Persist for at least seven days!

ALERT DIA-LOG: An Early Warning System

Your main purpose in learning ALERT DIA-LOG is that early warning signals help you recognize and become aware of harmful self-talk. Defeating dialogue usually leads to self-defeating behavior. It is in your best interest, therefore, to start challenging defeating dialogue in order to get the facts about what you are telling yourself.

One way to do this is to consider all "global" statements untrue until proved otherwise. *Global* statements are those that contain key alerts such as "should," "ought," "must," "always," "never," and similar words. Globals are overgeneralizations that are usually self-defeating.

Defeating dialogue comes from many things you have learned to believe are true. Although you will probably have to surrender some of your well-learned beliefs, opinions, and attitudes before you conquer most self-defeating behavior, you can *begin* by challenging your defeating self-talk. Defeating dialogue, such as "If I don't have the love of John/Jane it will be terrible and I'll never find another love," is an alert you can learn to challenge and replace with defensive dialogue. The defensive dialogue technique of managing stress and controlling self-defeating behavior is a sort of "no fault" therapeutic insurance. You stop faulting yourself and others for emotional behavior because it serves no purpose.

Begin to keep a log of the number of times a day you use the alert words listed below. These words are self-defeating and serve no good purpose.

TERM	*NUMBER OF TIMES USED*	*WAS TERM PRECEDED BY I, You, It, or They?*
MUST (or must not)		
SHOULD (or should not)		
HORRIBLE		
TERRIBLE		
NOBODY		
ALWAYS		
NEVER		
NONE		
UNFAIR		
DESERVE(D)		
ALL		
AWFUL		
NEED		
HAVE TO		
CAN'T STAND		
NO GOOD		
HOW DARE ________ !		
WHY TRY?		
EVERYBODY		
FOREVER		
NOTHING		

You may become aware of other alert words you are using, which you can add to this list. Make a contract with yourself now!

---

*CONTRACT FOR LEARNING ALERT WORDS
AND ALERT DIA-LOGS*

I agree to learn ALERT WORDS and ALERT DIA-LOGS. I will spend twenty minutes per day learning the ALERT WORDS and ALERT DIA-LOGS in this unit.

I will begin learning ALERT WORDS and ALERT

DIA-LOGS on (date): _______________________________

I will complete my learning by (date): _______________

Time of day I will study: _______________________

My reward for completing the terms of my contract is:

____

My penalty for not completing the terms of my contract is:

____

_________________________   _________________________
Witness' signature   My signature

                                          ____
                                          Date

You can learn to recognize self-talk that is damaging to your emotional well-being. Practice until you can catch yourself using defeating dialogue. Listed below are some self-statements you should start changing. They are statements based on crooked thinking, irrational beliefs, and unverifiable assumptions.

These alerts warn you that defeating dialogue threatens

and you are probably going to behave in a self-defeating way. Note the global, overgeneralized, commanding, demanding, judgmental nature of the statements.

> "I *can't* live without YIT (You/It/Them)."
> "I can't do that and it's *terribly unfair* for YIT to ask me!"
> "You *should love* me as much as I love you."
> "I *can't stand* for YIT to reject me!"
> "If I don't get that job my *future will be ruined!*"
> "YIT is *no good* and *should* be punished!"
> "*How dare* YIT criticize me!"
> "I'm locked into this boring job *forever.*"
> "*If this job* and my boss were more exciting I would not be so uhappy!"
> "YIT's *always* criticizing me."
> "I failed last time and I'll just *keep failing.*"
> "I *never* win."
> "I'm just a *born loser.*"
> "There is *nothing* about this job that I like."
> "If you cared *anything* about me you wouldn't have to ask how I feel!"
> "*If you loved me* I wouldn't have to ask you to do that."

Now test yourself by underlining the *alert words* in the following statements.

> "Nobody likes me."
> "I should get a raise because I deserve it."
> "YIT (You/It/They) should understand me."
> "If I don't get back at YIT it will show I'm weak."
> "When I ask for ______ I always get refused."
> "I couldn't stand to ask that!"
> "I'm no good at doing that."
> "YIT must be right and I must be wrong."
> "I always lose when I play that game."
> "Nobody ever invites me to lunch."
> "I'll never be able to afford a (vacation/car/house)."

"Salespeople always treat me rudely."
"I never know what to say."
"I always get stuck with the boring jobs."
"I deserve to be happy."
"Nobody understands me."
"I never get a good seat in a restaurant."
"I'll never finish this."
"I'd just die if I had to ask for a ____________."
"Just my luck. I'm always getting taken advantage of!"
"Everything bad happens to me."
"You don't really mean that. You're just being nice."
"This (*something good*) will never happen again."
"I'll be depressed forever. I'll never change."
"How terrible and awful that I made that mistake!"
"I feel unattractive, so I must be."
"It's all my fault. I'm just a bad (mother/father/child)."
"I must make a decision about my career right now or it
      will be too late for me."
"Everybody else my age (has a degree; is married; has a
      good job; knows)."
"If I goof up I'll lose their respect." (And, "I must have
      their respect.")
"I've never achieved much so I'm not much of a person."
"I must have their approval or I'll be terribly unhappy."
"I should do it because they expect it of me."
"There must be something wrong with me or YIT wouldn't
      reject me."
"He/she doesn't love me as I love him/her, so there must
      be something wrong with me."
"For me to be a worthwhile individual, I must be truly
      outstanding in some major area."
"I simply can't control the way I feel."
"I can't be happy because of all the bad things that have
      happened to me."
"Most people aren't ever happy."
"Most other people seem to be happy all the time."
"Bad things never happen to others like they do to me."
"I just don't have any confidence in myself and I'm sure
      I never will."

LEARNING HOW TO CHALLENGE DEFEATING DIALOGUE

Learning how to *challenge* defeating dialogue can seem quite a task. It takes recognition, practice, and persistence. You must learn to recognize *what* to challenge. You must be sure that you challenge your defeating dialogue, *not* what you *feel*. Once you recognize that it is what you say to yourself that causes the upsetting feeling, then you are on your way to controlling self-defeating behavior.

The challenge requires that you play the defense lawyer with yourself. Once you recognize the defeating dialogue, ask yourself probing questions about the statements you are making to yourself. In other words, raise doubts about the admissibility of the "evidence" you are presenting to "prove" your defeating dialogue. You have already learned the words and statements that alert you and remind you that a logical *defense* must be brought forth. Now you are going to ask for *proof*. Hearsay evidence is not acceptable. What you "feel" is not proof.

For now, all you need to learn is this: If you feel emotionally terrible, awful, depressed, outraged, or whatever, take a judicious look at the *dialogue* you had with yourself just before the feeling. Then, just as if you were charged with a crime, ask for proof of the validity of that dialogue.

Again, be sure you challenge the defeating *dialogue* and not the feeling. Question your self-talk as if you were an outsider. Practice being the outsider. Ask yourself, "What would I tell a friend who is becoming depressed as a result of this kind of unprovable defeating dialogue?"

Below are some examples of challenges that you should learn. Study them for a few minutes each day for two weeks. Start now to practice these challenges when you find yourself using defeating dialogue. Make a contract with yourself now!

1. Where is the proof for what I'm telling myself?
2. As long as I continue this dialogue, how will I feel?
3. If I tell myself something less severe, how will I feel?
4. What would I tell a friend who was using this self-talk?

   5. Is what I'm telling myself very good proof?
   6. Why *must* I?
   7. Why *should* YIT (You/It/They)?
   8. Why does it *have* to be?
   9. Where is this etched in stone?
10. If this is true, what is the *worst* thing that can happen?
11. Why does something unpleasant have to be *horrible*?
12. What's wrong with telling myself "I deserve it"?
13. Why is it impossible for me to predict that this will happen?
14. Why is this defeating dialogue?
15. How do they/I *know*?
16. What does this mean to me?

CONTRACT FOR LEARNING HOW TO CHALLENGE
DEFEATING DIALOGUE

I agree to learn how to challenge defeating dialogue.

I will begin to study these challenges on (date): ________

I will complete my learning by (date): ____________

I will practice these challenges at least ten minutes a day

for the next ___________________________ days.

Time of day I will study: ____________________

My reward for completing the terms of my contract is:

____

My penalty for not completing the terms of my contract is:

____

__________________	__________________
Witness' signature	My signature
	__________________
	Date

Below are some examples of how to challenge defeating dialogue.

1. *Where is the proof for what I'm telling myself?*
   "What research supports this belief? According to whom? Given the same situation, why don't all people believe this? Does this happen a hundred times out of a hundred?"

2. *As long as I continue this dialogue, how will I feel?*
   "Will I feel better? If I will not feel better, what purpose does this self-talk serve? Do I want to do myself in? It appears that it is not in my best interest to use this self-defeating dialogue. Under no condition will I feel good thinking this."

3. *If I tell myself something less severe, how will I feel?*
   "Instead of telling myself that this is the end of the world, how about calling it an unfortunate situation? I don't like it, but it isn't life-ending. I can change it for the better. It's sad, not catastrophic."

4. *Why should YIT?*
   "Is there a law that says YIT should do what I demand? YIT will do it only if YIT wants to. Really, YIT can do what YIT jolly well pleases. YIT doesn't *have* to."

5. *Why must I?*
   "According to what universal law? Where is it written that I *must*? Specifically, what authority is demanding that I must?"

6. *How do I know? How can I predict that?*
   "I'm not a fortune teller. I don't know for sure. It is impossible for me to predict the future, or what someone thinks."

You are now learning how you can change your self-defeating thoughts or defeating dialogue. It is important to remember that *you are in control.* You now have a choice.

Do not look outside yourself! Your perception of the initiating event and the dialogue *you* have with yourself generates the feeling that causes your self-defeating behavior.

Learn to become inner-directed! You can change the way you think and talk to yourself.

Challenge defeating dialogue!

Learn to ask questions when you tell yourself you suspect that something may not be true.
>Where is the evidence for what I just told myself?
>Where is the proof for what I just told myself?
>How do I know?

One technique of challenge is to determine the *real meaning* of a situation.

Below is an example of how to do this. Always challenge the dialogue, or talk, *not* the feeling. You already know how you feel—"awful," "terrible," "depressed," etc. Since self-defeating dialogue is responsible for your feeling, you want to *defend* yourself against the dialogue that precipitates the feeling.

1. *"My boss is not as friendly as before."*
   "Why does that upset me? What does it mean to me?"
2. *"It means that my boss doesn't like my work."*
   "If true, what does that mean to me?"
3. *"That means I'm not doing my job like other people here."*
   "And if true, what does that mean to me?"
4. *"That means that my pride is hurt."*
   "And if my pride is hurt, what does that mean to me?"
6. *"I take pride in my pride and I can't stand it."*
   "Suppose that is true. What is the worst thing that can happen?"

As you can see, if you continue to challenge your defeating dialogue you will eventually get to the *real meaning* of the situation instead of simply reacting emotionally. You will learn to defend yourself against the self-defeating dialogue, brought about by your illogical, unprovable, irrational thoughts, beliefs, attitudes, and opinions, that causes your emotional feelings.

In the preceding dialogue, for example, you soon realize that (1) you are *assuming* the boss doesn't like you; (2) it is really your pride you are concerned about and you are making an illogical attack on your pride—even if it is true that you *must* protect your pride; and, (3) assuming your pride *is* involved, what is the *worst* thing that can happen if it is hurt? Will you die? Will your arm drop off? The point is, it is perhaps *unfortunate* and you don't *like* it when your pride is hurt, but it is hardly catastrophic. The defensive dialogue, "It is unfortunate," is less emotionally upsetting than, "It is *awful* and I will *not stand* for it!" Because you feel better when you are not emotionally upset, you are in a psychological position to *change* the situation if that seems appropriate.

Practice how to reach the *meaning* of a situation. Once the process becomes a habit, you will have greater control over your self-defeating behavior. You will soon automatically recognize the thoughts, beliefs, and attitudes that contribute to the defeating dialogue that causes you to feel upset. Defensive dialogue will replace defeating dialogue which will increase the probability of an agreeable outcome.

Keep in mind that you aren't giving up your emotions. You are not becoming emotion-*less*. You are, rather, learning to respond with *appropriate* feelings, based on the realities of the situation. You are learning to defend yourself against the self-defeating dialogue that results from faulty assessment of an event and destructive self-talk. You are really not giving up a single thing—except a little time to learn! What you are doing is putting yourself in *control,* and *learning* to be appropriately, healthily, and rationally emotional.

CHECKLIST

I have completed or agree to complete the following learning assignments. I understand that I cannot go to the next unit until all blanks are checked.

_______________________________   _______________________________
          Signature   Date

__________ I can define "defeating dialogue."

__________ I can determine when my dialogue is defeating.

__________ I understand and can recognize ALERT WORDS and DIA-LOG.

__________ I am now, or will begin, keeping a log of ALERT WORDS.

__________ I am becoming familiar with techniques to challenge defeating dialogue.

__________ I must challenge defeating dialogue because it usually makes me feel bad.

DEFENDING, COPING, AND CHANGING

PURPOSE:
(1) To defend yourself against defeating dialogue
(2) to learn defensive dialogue
(3) to learn how to change

Defense: The best defense is a good defense!

If called upon to defend yourself against a fly, you would use a fly swatter or an appropriate insect repellent.

If called upon to defend yourself from an intruder into your house, you might use a gun or other suitable weapon.

If called upon to defend against an atomic bomb attack, a country might call for an atomic retaliatory strike.

The point is to choose a defense appropriate to the attack. If you want to get rid of a fly, you do not unleash an atomic arsenal against it. Accurate assessment of the initiating event is, therefore, essential for an appropriate response.

What you tell yourself about the attack will probably determine how you *feel* about that attack. It will also probably determine how you respond, or *behave*, toward the attack.

Recognizing when self-talk is an attack upon your well-being requires an alert system that warns you early of an imminent self-defeating attack. You must learn to challenge, and to defend yourself against, defeating dialogue if you are to cope with the events of your life sanely and healthfully.

You have now begun to recognize the ways you talk to yourself that result in self-defeating behavior. It is now apparent that you must defend yourself from defeating dialogue because it serves no purpose except to guarantee that you will feel bad.

You will now learn how to replace defeating dialogue with *defensive* dialogue.

> *Defensive dialogue consists of rational, verifiable self-statements that most probably lead to appropriate feelings, actively coping with situations, and positive outcomes.*

CONTRACT FOR LEARNING
TO REPLACE DEFEATING DIALOGUE
WITH DEFENSIVE DIALOGUE

I agree to learn to replace defeating dialogue with defensive dialogue, which includes *memorizing* the definition of Defensive Dialogue.

I will begin learning to replace defeating dialogue with defensive dialogue on (date): ___________________

I will complete my learning by (date): ___________________

Time of day I will study: ___________________

My reward for completing the terms of my contract is:

____

My penalty for not completing the terms of my contract is:

____

_______________________   _______________________

     Witness' signature   My signature

                                    ____

                                            Date

DETERMINING IF DIALOGUE IS DEFEATING OR DEFENSIVE

It is necessary to know whether your self-talk is defeating or defensive. You have learned some techniques that *help* you recognize defeating dialogue. Below are some criteria you can use to determine if your dialogue is defensive. Contract with yourself to spend one hour learning the material on pages 66–72.

1. Defensive dialogue reflects thoughts, opinions, and beliefs that are consistent with reality. The dialogue agrees with statements that can be proved, are logical, etc.
2. Defensive dialogue does not demand an absolute stand on an event (you must; it or I should; they ought). Instead, the self-talk usually expresses preferences or desires, and is moderate in content—for example, "I wish"; "it would be nice"; "I would prefer."
3. Defensive dialogue leads to appropriate feelings that allow you to cope, rather than emotions that upset you and lead to self-defeating behavior. "I don't like what happened. Let's see what I can do to change it."
4. Defensive dialogue is characterized by positive statements which usually make you feel better, since they are based on reality, and help you avoid the "poor-me syndrome" or the "damn-you syndrome." Defensive dialogue helps you reach the desirable goal of more happiness and less emotional conflict. "I don't *always* lose. I'll see what I need to do to turn this around."

DEFENDING AGAINST DEFEATING DIALOGUE

OBJECTIVE: To learn how to recognize self-defeating dialogue and to replace it with defensive dialogue.

Defeating dialogues are statements you make to yourself that very probably make you feel bad. They serve no good purpose. They are not based on reason or rationality. You have learned to talk to yourself in a defeating way. You must give this up because it is self-defeating.

The core elements of reason-*less* beliefs that precede defeating dialogue are the following:

1. YIT STATEMENTS ("*You*," "*It*," "*They*" Dialogue)
   This dialogue reflects the belief that there are absolute and universal *musts*. "YIT *should* or *must* do such-and-such" or "YIT *has to* or *ought to* do something."

DEFEATING DIALOGUE	DEFENSIVE DIALOGUE
(look for *YIT* statements)	
"You should _________ "	"Why? It would be nice, but _________ "
"I should or it should _________ "	"I'd like _________ "
"They should _________ "	"Only if they choose to. There's no law that says they *must*."

2. ACT STATEMENTS ("*Awful*," "*Catastrophic*," and "*Terrible*" Dialogue)
   This dialogue tells you that *Awful, Catastrophic,* and *Terrible* (ACT) things in this world happen to you! They are more than deplorable, unfortunate, sad, or regrettable. They are simply unbearable!

DEFEATING DIALOGUE	DEFENSIVE DIALOGUE
(look for *ACT* statements)	
"It's just awful!"	"How deplorable!"
"It's catastrophic!"	"It's unfortunate."
"It's simply terrible!"	"I regret it."

3. NEED DIALOGUE
   This dialogue reflects your belief that you *need* and *must* have certain things in this world or you may die! You are convinced that the need is necessary for your survival!

DEFEATING DIALOGUE	DEFENSIVE DIALOGUE
(these are similar to shoulds)	
"I need her/him."	"It's nice to have his/her love and affection."
"I need the promotion."	"I want the promotion, but the world won't end if . . . ."

4. WORTHINESS DIALOGUE
   This self-talk reflects your belief that a person's worth as a human being (yourself included) can be judged on some kind of scale.

DEFEATING DIALOGUE	DEFENSIVE DIALOGUE
"I am no good."	"Many things about me are good. Maybe my behavior could be improved, but I do many good things."
"You're not good." "It's not good." "They're no good." (these are YIT statements)	"I don't like what just happened, but I can't rate YIT's behavior as all bad based on one or two specific actions. If this is really indicative of YIT's behavior, then I may choose to stay away from YIT."

Practice saying *stop!* to yourself when defeating dialogue comes into your thoughts. Color *stop!* red in your imagination if you wish. Immediately after you say *stop!* start replacing the defeating dialogue with defensive dialogue. For example:

"What a horrible day. Everything bad happens to me!" (defeating dialogue)

"Stop!"

"Hey, everything hasn't gone wrong. Some nice things have happened. I was able to get up this morning! My health could be much worse." (Learn to make lists of *good* things. Always think of the good things. Write them down.)

"How dare that person reject me!" (defeating dialogue)

"Stop!"

"People can reject me if they choose. No one's obliged by some law to do what I want." (defensive dialogue)

"But I can't *stand* rejection." (defeating dialogue)

"Stop!"

"Yes I can. It won't kill me. Let's see what I can do to change this situation." (defensive dialogue)

"But this person is *always* doing something like this!" (defeating dialogue)

"Stop!"

"*Always* is too global and overgeneral. It is true that this person often seems to reject me. Maybe I'll explore this and determine if this is the kind of person for me." (defensive dialogue)

FIVE STEPS TO EMOTIONAL DEFENSE

This diagram shows you how defensive dialogue results in a positive outcome.

EXAMPLE: *The Initiating Event:* I have been excluded from a party by my coworkers.

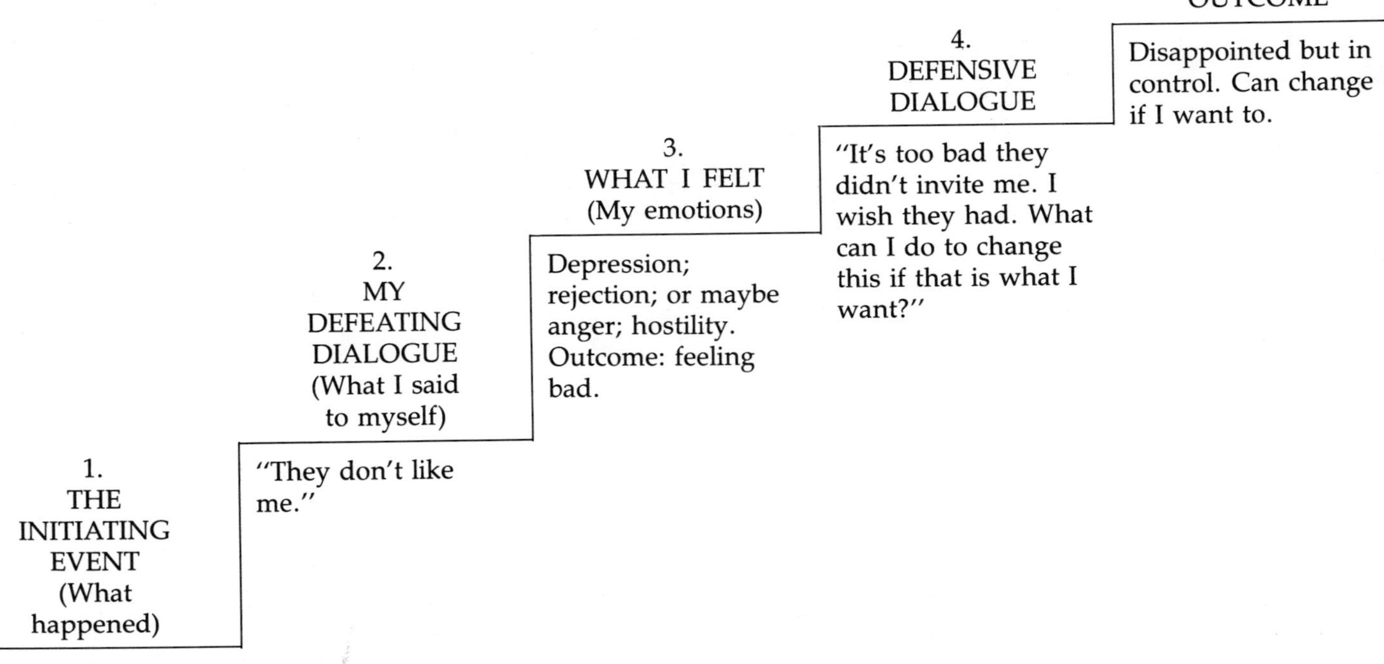

LEARNING DEFENSIVE DIALOGUE

OBJECTIVE: To learn to replace defeating dialogue with defensive dialogue.

DEFEATING DIALOGUE (Terms to give up)	*PRACTICE SAYING*	*DEFENSIVE DIALOGUE* (Replacement dialogue)
"I can't *stand* it!"	*Stop!*	"It's unfortunate, but not deadly."
"It's horrible!"	*Stop!*	"I'd rather it were different, but the world won't end. It's quite bearable."
"I *never* win."	*Stop!*	"Nonsense! I often win. 'Never' is ridiculous!"
"I just can't live without ________ ."	*Stop!*	"Then why don't other people in this situation die? Out of *all the* people in the world I know I can find *one*."
"I simply *must*!"	*Stop!*	"Why *must* I? Suppose I don't; what is the worst thing that can happen?"
"(You) (It) (They) ought to ________ ." (It's YIT's fault!)	*Stop!*	"Where is it written that YIT has that *duty*? How can I demand that of YIT?"
"This is just *awful*!"	*Stop!*	"If I continue to believe that, how will I *feel*? Then why should I believe it?"
"It's *unfair*!"	*Stop!*	"Sure, there is unfairness in the world. But it is not to my

		advantage to get angry about it. Anger is self-defeating. It's unfortunate, but I refuse to get angry."
"What a *horrible* day!"	*Stop!*	"Wait just a minute! *Everything* hasn't gone wrong—just a couple of things." (Make a list of things that are nice.)
"*Nobody* loves me."	*Stop!*	"Baloney! I have friends and family. If I want more love then I'll start working on this. For example, I'll learn to think more positively."
"I *hate* ________ !"	*Stop!*	"Hating makes me feel bad. I don't like ________ , but I refuse to hate because it is self-defeating. I can't change things for the better by hating."
"There will *never* be another chance like this."	*Stop!*	"How do I *know* that? Am I a fortune teller? Even if true, what will happen?"
"I'll *never* be a success!"	*Stop!*	"That's absurd! I can't predict that based on this one failure. What can I do—starting right now—to rethink my definition of success?"
"It's just *terrible* that I failed."	*Stop!*	"It was a disappointment that I didn't get that job. I'll try to find out what went wrong."

"This traffic is *horrible.* I'll never get to work on time!"	*Stop!*	"All this traffic certainly is annoying. I'll start leaving home a few minutes earlier."
"How dare my boss yell at me! I can't *stand* it anymore."	*Stop!*	"I get very uncomfortable when my boss yells at me. What can I do to change this?"
"I *must* get that job or I'll be a failure."	*Stop!*	"If I want to get that job I'll find out what the requirements are. If I don't get the job I'll learn what it takes for next time."

CONTRACT FOR ASSIGNMENT 1:
DAILY DIA-LOG: THINKING DEFENSIVELY

I agree to practice and complete Assignment 1.

____

____

I will begin on (date): _______________________

I will finish on (date): _______________________

The time of day I will study is: _______________
(Recommended time: one day for one hour.)

My reward for learning this assignment is: ______

____

My penalty for not learning this assignment is: ________

____

_______________________　　_______________________
　　Witness' signature　　　　　　　My signature

　　　　　　　　　　　　　　_______________________
　　　　　　　　　　　　　　　　　　　Date

ASSIGNMENT 1: DAILY DIA-LOG: THINKING DEFENSIVELY

Keep a daily record of all upsetting events and emotions until you can automatically think defensively.

THE EVENT	MY SELF-TALK (Defeating Dialogue)	MY FEELING	I CAN REPLACE DEFEATING DIALOGUE WITH:

Now go back to your *Daily Stress and Tension Log* (see page 43). After you have logged your stressors and responses for several days (at least a week is recommended), begin to develop a *Stress Defense Log* in the following manner.

1. Continue to record what happened to cause you stress.
2. Continue to become familiar with your self-talk, which is probably *defeating dialogue.*
3. Replace this stressful, ineffective, defeating dialogue with relaxed and effective *defensive dialogue.*

The techniques of defensive dialogue can be used to defend yourself against specific stressors. Now that you are in touch with what actually happens to stress you and what you say to yourself in response, you can replace the stressful, defeating dialogue with coping, defensive dialogue.

WHAT HAPPENED TO STRESS ME (*initiating event*)	*WHAT I SAID TO MYSELF* (*stressful, defeating dialogue*)	*WHAT I COULD SAY TO MYSELF* (*coping, defensive dialogue*)
1. 7:45 A.M. Got up 45 minutes late.	Rushed around madly. Said to myself, "I just can't be late. That would be awful. My day will be ruined. I'll get nothing done."	"I'm not often late. I'll just call in and say I'm running late. It's no problem. I'll make up the time."
	OUTCOME: Stress. Leave in a hurry. Keep telling myself terrible things.	*OUTCOME:* Less stress. Effective coping and management.

2. 8:15 A.M. Big traffic jam. Driver in front won't move over.

   "Why doesn't that idiot move over? HEY! GET OVER, MISTER! I can't stand drivers like that!"

   OUTCOME; Stress; heart beats fast; blood pressure rises; arrive at work in bad shape.

   "I don't like this but I can't do anything about it now. Since traffic is so slow, I'll plan my day and be more effective."

   OUTCOME: Low stress. Using time effectively for planning. More relaxed.

3. 10:30 P.M. Can't go to sleep.

   "What a horrible day. I was late. Didn't get much accomplished. I don't deserve this!"

   OUTCOME: Stress keeps sleep away. Feel exhausted and depressed.

   "My planning made for an effective day. I did a good day's work."

   OUTCOME: Good night's sleep. Awoke feeling good.

DEVELOPING STRESS MANAGEMENT SKILLS

Stress is a part of life. Every day we find ourselves confronted with situations that evoke stress responses. It is to each person's advantage, therefore, to know how to cope with stress.

Managing stress effectively is a *learned* skill. Anything learned requires *practice*. Thus, if you are to learn stress management skills you *must* practice. You can do it! It is a matter of deciding that you are going to master a skill that is of basic and vital importance to your general well-being and to your ability to live fully and productively in a stress-filled world.

The following drills will help you manage stress. *Practice* each one daily until they are a habitual part of your everyday behavior. *Make a contract now!*

CONTRACT FOR LEARNING STRESS MANAGEMENT SKILLS

I agree to learn stress management techniques.

I will begin learning these skills on (date): ______________

I will complete my learning by (date): ______________

My schedule will be as follows:
Days of the week I will study: ______________

Time of day I will study: ______________

Total time each week I will study: ______________

My reward for completing the terms of my contract is:

____

My penalty for not completing the terms of my contract is:

____

<table>
<tr><td>___________________
Witness' signature</td><td>___________________
My signature

____
Date</td></tr>
</table>

STRESS DESENSITIZATION EXERCISE

You can reduce the intensity of certain stress activating events through a Stress Densensitization Exercise (SDE). Its purpose is to increase your ability to cope with stress by thinking about a stressful situation and practicing defensive dialogue to counteract your defeating thoughts. The stress log presented earlier is an example of an SDE.

You may want to practice an SDE with one or more friends. You can devise your own exercise, but the techniques used in defensive dialogue should be helpful.

Before starting an SDE, create a contract that outlines your goals, when you will practice, and the rewards that follow completion of your SDE.

Remember, you are attempting to cope with stress by *challenging* or redefining what you tell yourself about the stress initiating event. You are learning to *question* what you say to yourself.

An SDE involves four steps.

1. Awareness of stress.
2. Challenging the stress initiating event.
3. Coping with the stress.
4. Rewarding yourself for coping with the stress.

The following self-talk is an example of an SDE.

Q = The question you ask yourself.
A = The answer you give to the question.

Q. "How can I tell that stress is threatening?"
A. "I feel upset. I'm about to get a headache."

Q. "What am I saying to myself at this time?"
A. "That I can't handle this. That awful things are about to happen to me."
Q. "What proof do I have that I can't handle this?"
A. "I just don't *think* I can."
Q. "But, that is only what I *think*. What proof do I have that this is unbearable?"
A. "None, really. I just believe it!"
Q. "What can I do to relieve this stress?"
A. "Tell myself that the world won't end because of this. I have no proof that this is really catastrophic. I won't die if I do not handle it perfectly."
Q. "Sure, but how do I actually reduce the stress?"
A. "I can use a deep relaxation drill and imagine myself listening to a cool, blue, running brook."
"I can say '*no!*' if I begin to feel stress while trying to relax."
"I can say to myself, 'What's the good of getting upset—that *never* works.'"
Q. "How can I be sure that I will continue to progress in my stress management?"
A. "By congratulating myself for fulfilling my contract and rewarding myself for persisting in learning stress management skills."

Always remember to incorporate the four-step process into your SDE:

1. Become aware of the stress initiating event.
2. Challenge the stress intitiating event and become better prepared mentally to cope.
3. Cope with the stress.
4. Reward yourself for actively coping and managing stress.

STRESS MANAGEMENT SKILLS

Deep muscle relaxation and mental relaxation are two skills important to your stress management program. Most people find these relaxation drills helpful and easy to learn. If you take blood pressure medication or have suffered from serious mental illness, do *not* begin a program of relaxation techniques without consulting your physician.

DEEP MUSCLE RELAXATION DRILL
1. Choose a quiet place where you can be comfortable in either a lying or sitting position.
2. Close your eyes; picture a quiet brook gently flowing through a lush garden.
3. Make a fist with your right hand—tighten your fist; now relax your fist and let your hand and fingers become loose.
4. Now instruct your arm to become very heavy and warm.
5. Next, relax the muscles in your right forearm, upper arm, and shoulder. Feel them become heavy and warm.
6. Now, relax your upper right leg, lower leg, and foot.
7. Next, follow the same procedure with your left fist, arm, leg, and foot.
8. Now relax the muscles in your hips. Let the relaxation flow into your stomach and chest. Relax, don't tense these muscles. Feel the warmth and heaviness.
9. Relax your breathing. Notice how slow and effortless your breathing is becoming.
10. Now relax your shoulders, neck, jaw, and facial muscles. Tell your forehead to be cool. Feel the coolness.

You may need some assistance in deep muscle relaxation drills. Some people have difficulty learning this drill because of mental interference. If you can't seem to achieve deep muscle relaxation, you may benefit from the following drill.

GETTING IN TOUCH WITH YOUR MUSCLES
1. Lie on your back in a quiet place and be as passive as possible.
2. Make every muscle in your body as *tense* as possible. Hold the tension for five seconds.
3. Let your muscles go as limp as you can.

4. Repeat this drill, then exhale very slowly as you relax your muscles. Go limp.
5. Be aware of your relaxed state. Now begin with step 3 of the muscle relaxation drill.

Memorize and then practice this drill for fifteen minutes in the morning and fifteen minutes in the afternoon. If you can't afford fifteen minutes, spend at least a few minutes twice a day. You may want to practice before a meal and especially before any anticipated stressful event. It's probably best, however, to limit yourself to about three drills a day.

After you have learned deep muscle relaxation, you are ready to learn how to clear your mind of stressful thoughts and manage your worries through mental relaxation. Before beginning the Mental Relaxation Drill, put yourself into a state of deep muscle relaxation.

MENTAL RELAXATION DRILL
1. Close your eyes. Clear the thoughts from your mind and achieve a passive state. If thoughts recur, whisper *stop* or *no* to yourself. Say it over and over if necessary, but remain in a state of muscle relaxation. If the thought seems to be receding, silently say *ah* to your now clear mind.
2. Imagery is an important part of this drill. For example, replace an unwanted thought with a picture of a lush garden with a blue waterfall in the background. Keep your eyes closed. See a beautiful blue sky. Say to yourself, "Beautiful, peaceful; I'm totally relaxed."
3. Think of your breathing—slowly inhale and exhale. Notice how your breathing is easy, slow, and effortless. Become aware of each breath—in and out. Say *no* to any interference. If you still have trouble relaxing say *ah* as you exhale.
4. Keep your facial muscles relaxed, your forehead cool.
5. Enjoy the mental relaxation for several minutes. If you don't feel calm, relaxed, and rested, repeat the drill.

One of the benefits of learning how to achieve deep muscle and mental relaxation is that you can transfer the techniques to shorter time periods. The instant relaxation drill will help you to enter a partial state of relaxation within one or two minutes. Follow these steps.

> *INSTANT RELAXATION DRILL*
> 1. Make yourself comfortable—whether you are sitting or standing in line, or just before a stress initiating event.
> 2. Take a deep breath and hold it for five seconds.
> 3. Exhale *slowly* while telling yourself to relax your muscles. (Specifically work on face, neck, and shoulder muscles.)
> 4. Repeat steps 2 and 3 five times.
> 5. If you are in a place where you can use imagery, picture a calm, pleasant scene such as a blue brook, lush garden, or deep blue skies.

Use this drill when defeating dialogue (which is a signal that stress is forthcoming) is present. Use the instant relaxation drill to reduce the intensity of stress initiating events.

Here's a breathing method to relieve distress temporarily:

> 1. Sit in a comfortable chair
> 2. Close your eyes
> 3. Do not cross your arms or legs
> 4. Attend to your breathing cycle for a few seconds
> 5. Inhale for three seconds
> 6. Hold the breath for twelve seconds
> 7. Exhale for six seconds
> 8. Do this about six or seven times and you will probably feel some stress relief.

CONTROLLING STRESS BY ALTERING THE STRESSOR CONDITION

> O God, give us serenity to accept what cannot be changed, courage to change what should be changed, and the wisdom to distinguish the one from the other.[1]

To live healthier, happier, and longer, you may need to take direct action on a stressor by reducing its intensity, removing it altogether, or redefining its consequences. Taking into account the fact that you have just so much adaptive energy, it is in your best interest to use it wisely. The following suggestions can help you to do this.

Reduce the stressor's intensity by:
1. Physical relaxation, and/or
2. Mental relaxation, and/or
3. Exercise, and/or
4. Rest, and/or
5. Controlling self-defeating behavior, thereby removing stress-inducing thoughts.

Remove the stressor by:
1. Mental imagery, and/or
2. Removal of defeating dialogue, and/or
3. Eliminating high risk behavior such as smoking, eating too much, drinking too much, and/or
4. Removing stress-inducing thoughts by controlling self-defeating behavior.

Redefine the stressor's consequences (that is, convince yourself that the situation is less critical than you have led yourself to believe) by:
1. Controlling self-defeating behavior, and/or
2. Mental imagery, and/or
3. Redefining stress inducing thoughts through controlling self-defeating behavior.

You will notice that some form of control of self-defeating thoughts and behavior is present in all of the direct actions upon stressors. It is important, then, that you learn to challenge the self-defeating thoughts that produce stress. These thoughts are usually a result of acquired illogical, irrational, and unhealthy responses to situations. The technique of learning and using defensive dialogue is an important stress management skill.

COPING

There are three ways to cope with almost any situation. All three result from your thinking processes. Two of the coping mechanisms result in *self-defeating* behavior. The consequences are also self-defeating.

In most situations you can choose one of three options: (1) the *poor me option;* (2) the *YIT (You/It/Them) option;* or (3) the *change option.* Since your emotional feelings are a result of what you believe the situation to be, your behavior and the outcome depend on the option *you* choose.

The *poor me option* applies to people who put themselves down, blame fate, accept all criticism as factual, and generally have a low self-concept. They never challenge their defeating dialogue or their accuser. They often label themselves losers, total failures, goof-ups, etc. Behaviorally, they are sad, depressed, withdrawn, passive, and anxious. The outcome is whining, low self-esteem, poor work habits, and poor relationships. These people probably are absent from work more, and are less productive than, the average person. They always *feel bad.* They make ACT statements: "Things are just Awful!" "I can't deal with this Catastrophe!"; "It's so Terrible, and I can't go on!"

The *YIT (You/It/Them) option* is characterized by blaming someone who had nothing to do with the situation—it was all caused by "You," "It," or "Them." YIT people never look inward. They never challenge the defeating dialogue which says, 'That stupid boss is on my case again," or, "If it weren't for them I'd be _______ ," or, "If so and so didn't such and such I wouldn't such and such." YIT people are usually frustrated and angry. Behaviorally, they cast accusations, blame "those responsible" for the situation, and are no fun to be around. YIT people get fired a lot, spend much of their time cursing the no-good world, don't get along on the job or at home, and generally *feel bad.* These people become victims of the YIT trap. Since they are not pleasant to be around, others avoid them, which in turn causes them to blame YIT even more.

People who choose the *change option* take the responsibility for making their situation better. If they aren't happy in a situation, they look for a way to change it. They ask themselves: what are the facts; what is the problem; what can *I* do here. They come up with a possible solution to the problem and act. Change people practice positive self-talk that discourages *self-defeating* behavior and helps them feel good. They learn *defensive dialogue.* They have high self-esteem, look for the facts (proof, evidence), and learn how to cope with the situation effectively and positively. They learn to think *rationally.* They learn how to *feel good!*

Most people can learn to change. Certainly *you* can. Coping with situations in this healthy way is not a trait that is passed through the genes to a lucky few; it is not the result of a vision in the night; it doesn't come as one lies on a psychiatrist's couch; it is not a result of a few minutes reading in a book about positive thinking.

Rational thinking, challenging defeating dialogue, and using defensive dialogue are learned. The ability to control self-defeating behavior is a result of practice and persistence, practice and persistence, practice and persistence—and patience.

DEVELOPING YOUR PERSONAL PLAN FOR STRESS MANAGEMENT AND CONTROLLING SELF-DEFEATING BEHAVIOR

The skills you have learned in this program—identifying stress problems, commitment by contract, awareness of stress, and stress management—can help you develop your own personal plan to control self-defeating behavior and manage stess. Though needs vary according to the individual, *all* plans should incorporate:

- Commitment to change
- The ability to recognize stressors
- Awareness of defeating dialogue
- Planning a week or two at a time
- Daily practice of mental and muscle relaxation drills
- Practice, persistence, and patience

CHECKLIST

I have completed or agree to complete the following assignments. I understand that by learning all units in this book I will be well on my way to managing stress and controlling self-defeating behavior.

_______________________________   _______________________________

          Signature   Date

__________ I can define defensive dialogue.

__________ I can recognize self-defeating dialogue and
replace it with defensive dialogue.

__________ I understand *YIT* statements.

__________ I understand *ACT* statements.

__________ I understand *need* statements.

__________ I understand *worthiness* statements.

__________ I can say *stop!* when I use defeating
dialogue.

__________ I am familiar with the three ways I can cope
with a situation.

__________ I will continue to practice the techniques I
have learned in this book.

CONCLUSION

You have now learned the techniques and methods of emotional
defense that enable you to manage stress and control self-defeating behavior. If you practice these techniques on a regular
basis, you will begin to take command of your life. The payoff is
less stress, anxiety, and depression, and increased happiness.

Now that you know the procedures for managing stress
and controlling self-defeating behavior, you will want to maintain
what you have achieved. Maintenance is much easier than the
initial change. However, you will need to review, reevaluate, and
revitalize your stress management program, and practice the basic
skills you have learned. A maintenance checklist, such as the one
shown below, may help as you continue to practice the techniques
of assessment, defensive dialogue, and muscle and mental relaxation.

In summary, continue to review:

1. How to recognize stressors and events that initiate your
   unsettling feelings,
2. How to identify your inner talk as defeating dialogue.
3. How to evaluate what emotions you feel from your
   defeating dialogue.
4. How to replace defeating dialogue with defensive dialogue, which will enable you to
5. Experience appropriate feelings, cope effectively, and
   manage stress.

MAINTENANCE CHECKLIST

Check the list below every day, every Monday of each week, and day one of every month. This checklist will help you maintain the skills you have learned.

DAILY First thing every morning I will:	WEEKLY Every Monday morning I will:	MONTHLY On day one of every month I will:
1. Begin with a positive, rational statement: "How nice it is to feel good."	1. Write a contract for at least one thing I want to work on.	1. Read "I'm Going to Manage Stress and Defend Myself Against Self-Defeating Behavior."
2. Practice at least one relaxation exercise for three minutes.	2. Review my stressors, and either reduce their intensity, change their intensity, or eliminate them.	2. Define and recognize defeating dialogue.
3. Say: "I feel the way I think."	3. Review my relaxation exercises.	3. Practice how to challenge defeating dialogue and replace it with defensive dialogue.
4. Say: "Rational thinking helps me feel good."	4. Review ALERT DIA-LOG and say "stop" when I use defeating dialogue.	4. Log stressors and unsettling events for at least one day.

5. If I wish something were different, say: "How can I change it?"

5. Begin, and continue all week, to assess initiating events accurately and objectively.

6. Practice stress reduction exercises.

5. Review YIT and ACT statements.

6. Review need and worthiness dialogue.

7. Review the unit on "Coping."

Most of all you will practice, persist, and be patient. What you have learned in this book *is* habit forming. What is more, it is a safe habit. You *are* in control, so go ahead—feel good!

NOTES
1.   This prayer was composed by Reinhold Neibuhr (1892–1971), and is widely used by a number of national and international organizations.

NOTES

NOTES

NOTES

NOTES

NOTES